"I am so stoked about this study! It's like the cheat code[...] your parents' study — nothing preachy, boring, or dorky here! It's filled with the goods to help you enjoy today and reach your future goals faster and easier. And it's filled with a bonus: Through it God will use you to rock our nation for His glory!"

— TONY NOLAN, author and evangelist

"*Josiah Road* is a valuable tool for every student leader who wants to leave an imprint on the next generation."

— BRENT CROWE, vice president, Student Leadership University

"*Josiah Road* is an engaging, fast-paced, winsome, and substantive tool to encourage a new generation of Christians to consider their obligations to the world in the name of the kingdom. It provokes both thought and action."

— RUSSELL D. MOORE, senior vice president, dean of the School of Theology,
The Southern Baptist Theological Seminary

"Throughout history, students have made a choice to lead movements that focused on the importance of chasing after God. This is what *Josiah Road* is all about!"

— ED STETZER, president, LifeWay Research

"*Josiah Road* connects the dots of purpose and passion with the Millennial generation."

— DR. JAY STRACK, president and founder, Student Leadership

"Luke and Harold Harper have teamed up to provide an incredible resource for students eager to wholly follow Christ. With the kind of rare insights and transparency that can come only from a father-son partnership, they show us what is possible for our lives, families, and futures if, like Josiah, we pursue God with passion and determination."

— TOM ELLIFF, president, International Mission Board, Southern Baptist Convention

"Creative! Compelling! Challenging! Inspiring! Transforming! All these and more superlatives accurately describe *Josiah Road*. It is a bridge to an emerging generation that can be used of God to captivate their hearts. You must read it, study it, and share it!"

— JIMMY DRAPER, former president, Southern Baptist Convention

"*Josiah Road* is a serious study about equipping a generation of students for taking a stand and influencing and leading out in today's culture."

— BRIAN MILLS, student pastor, Long Hollow Baptist Church, Hendersonville, Tennessee

STUDENT GUIDE

CALLED TO

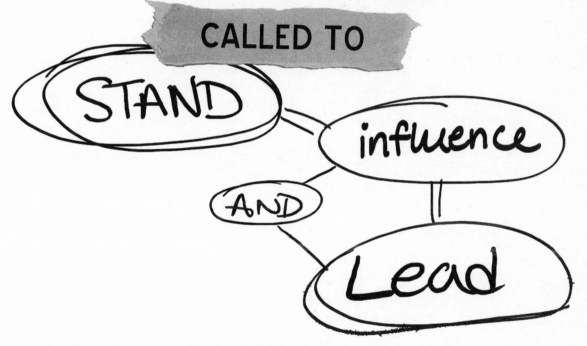

STAND

influence

AND

Lead

Luke & Harold Harper
with Rachel Lovingood

NAVPRESS

Discipleship Inside Out™

THINK

NAVPRESS
Discipleship Inside Out™

NavPress is the publishing ministry of The Navigators, an international Christian organization and leader in personal spiritual development. NavPress is committed to helping people grow spiritually and enjoy lives of meaning and hope through personal and group resources that are biblically rooted, culturally relevant, and highly practical.

For a free catalog go to www.NavPress.com
or call 1.800.366.7788 in the United States or 1.800.839.4769 in Canada.

ISBN-13: 978-1-61747-274-9 (student guide)

Cover design by The Resonate Group, Kerry Bural

Printed in the United States of America

1 2 3 4 5 6 7 8 / 16 15 14 13 12 11

This book is dedicated to the wonderful new addition to our family, Josiah James Harper. Love you, little brother!

Dear Friend,

You are about to set out on one of the most exciting journeys of all time: becoming part of a new generation of leaders who take a bold stand for the Lord Jesus!

If you really desire to see Jesus make a difference — in your life and the lives of your family, your church, your community, and your country — you will be encouraged as you study the life of Josiah.

Set aside a specific time and place every day to study each day's assignment. The seriousness of this material dictates that you approach it thoughtfully and purposefully. Take the time to enjoy the study instead of rushing through it and trying to complete several days in one sitting.

Always begin your study time in prayer. Ask God to open your understanding to the Scripture (see Luke 24:45). Try to memorize the key verse of every lesson (see Psalm 119:15).

If you lack the assurance that Jesus Christ is truly your Lord and Savior, please don't begin this study until you turn to page 97 so you can discover what it means to have a relationship with Jesus Christ. Unless you are a believer, this study will be just empty words on pages and have little value for your life.

We pray that as you work through these sessions, this journey would be more than merely a study of the Scriptures to increase your knowledge about the Bible. Our hope is that God will use this study to change your heart and life, thus deepening your relationship with Him.

Keep the faith,

Richard Land
President and CEO
Ethics & Religious Liberty Commission

For the kingdom,

Dr. Jay Strack
President
Student Leadership University

Contents

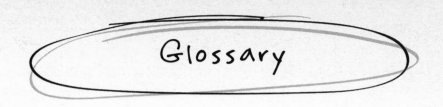

Glossary

Amon:
Josiah's father. Such an evil king that his servants killed him.

Crossroad:
A place where two or more roads intersect. A time when important changes occur or major decisions must be made. A crucial point.

David:
Josiah's ancestor, the king of Israel, who did what was right in the Lord's sight. Josiah followed David's example.

Hilkiah:
Priest who found the Book of the Law of the Lord (written by Moses) when King Josiah ordered the temple to be restored.

Josiah:
Became king of Jerusalem when he was eight years old and reigned for thirty years (640–609 BC). Josiah did what was right in the Lord's sight and walked in the ways of his ancestor David. He did not turn aside to the right or the left.

Lessons from the Journey:
Stories from students who are seeking God and sharing lessons they are learning along the way as they follow Christ.

Manasseh:
Josiah's grandfather. An evil king who angered God.

Memory Verse:
Passages from the Bible you will want to memorize. Use the Scripture memory cards on page 95 for help.

Mile Marker:

A marker set up on a roadside to indicate the distance in miles from a given point. Mile Markers in this study are designed to define terms that will help you during this study.

Off-Road Challenge:

An extra test of one's abilities. Off-Road Challenges in this study are optional and designed for the student who wants to go deeper in the study of God's Word.

Road Warrior:

One who is engaged aggressively or energetically in an activity, cause, or conflict. Road Warriors in this study are those who have decided to make a difference for Christ while they are still young.

Speed Bump:

The purpose of a speed bump is to reduce the speed of vehicles traveling along a roadway and cause drivers to slow down and take notice. During this study you are encouraged to slow down and think about what God is trying to say to you as you work through the content.

Suggested Tunes for the Journey:

Suggested songs you may want to listen to as you work through this study. These songs have been chosen because they relate to specific subjects.

Travel Tip:

A piece of advice or inside information given by an experienced Christ follower.

Yield Sign:

Indicates to drivers that they must yield the right-of-way, slow down, or stop; to give up control.

Meet the Authors

Luke and Harold Harper

Thanks for picking up a copy of *Josiah Road*. My name is Luke Harper. My family — my dad, Harold; my mom, Donna; my sister, Hannah; my brother, Josiah; and our dog, Copper — lives in Hendersonville, Tennessee.

My dad is executive vice president of the Southern Baptist Convention's Ethics & Religious Liberty Commission and cohost of the radio broadcast *For Faith & Family*. He spends a lot of his time speaking, teaching, and pouring himself into others.

I'm a high school student in Nashville. I play three sports: football, basketball, and soccer. I spend most of my time at school, in the gym, or at church.

I love to write. In my free time I watch ESPN, the Dallas Mavericks, the LSU Tigers, and the Tennessee Titans. I like playing video games and volleyball and "chillaxin" with my friends. I love road trips, youth trips, mission trips, pancakes, pasta, and sweet tea.

Rachel Lovingood

Mrs. Rachel has a degree in mass communications and journalism from Louisiana Tech University. She is a published author and freelance writer. She is married to my student pastor, Jeff Lovingood, and they have three cool kids: Trevor, Kelsey, and Riley. Like many parents, she spends a lot of time sitting on bleachers. We all attend Long Hollow Baptist Church in Hendersonville, Tennessee.

Thanks for your willingness to journey alongside me and my dad through the study of Josiah!

—Luke Harper

Introduction

The other day my dad went to Starbucks for some TAWG (time alone with God). As soon as he walked in, he noticed that he wasn't the only one hanging out there to study the Bible. Across the room were two students with their Bibles open. Nothing unusual about these guys . . . jeans, T-shirts, flip-flops, backpacks. They appeared to be very good friends, and my dad got the impression that this was not the first time they had studied together.

My dad sat down across the room with his iPod, journal, and Bible. Soon he was jamming with Matt Papa and into God's Word. But for some reason, these two guys kept catching his attention. They were laughing and seemed to be having a great time, even though my dad couldn't hear a word they were saying.

About halfway through his TAWG, my dad looked up and noticed that one of them had his face in his hands and appeared to be upset. Dad tried not to stare, but they had his complete attention. (Admit it: A guy crying in Starbucks would get your attention too.)

It was clear that this guy was dealing with some heavy stuff. But it was not the guy crying that my dad was watching — it was his friend.

Here they were in a busy store full of people lined up to get their morning fix. But these guys were oblivious to the crowd. The one not crying was completely focused on his hurting friend — so focused, in fact, that he got up and stood beside him and starting praying. It blew my dad away. What a bold move! The guys didn't seem to care where they were or that they had an audience. The one standing didn't seem to be embarrassed by his hurting friend.

My dad couldn't take his eyes off them. This guy was standing there so confident, so sure of himself. He didn't say a word. Yet my dad knew he was a guy who spent time with God because he saw Christ at work through him.

Don't you wish you had friends like that? Don't you wish you could be that kind of friend? I long to be a friend like that and to have friends like that! I think it would be cool to have a group of friends who were so committed that they would literally stand for God even in a busy Starbucks.

Over the past four years, my dad and I have been studying different people in the Bible who took a stand for God. Josiah is one who caught our attention.

Josiah was an absolute beast (pretty radical). At the age of eight, he started running a small country. He didn't waste time; he didn't wait till he was older to start leading. He used his influence to take a stand and lead his nation back to God.

During these five sessions, you are going to explore some "nation-leading" skills. You will be challenged to take a hard look at what is around you and evaluate where you are headed. You will be asked to examine what's hindering your relationship with Christ. You'll be asked to determine what GPS you are going to use to guide you along the way.

I'm not going to lie to you. This is hard stuff! You will be challenged to take risks, seize opportunities, defy the odds, and pursue God's purpose for your life like never before. Get ready to travel Josiah's Road!

—Luke Harper

SESSION 1
ACCELERATE:
What Drives You?

Josiah was eight years old when he became king; he reigned 31 years in Jerusalem. He did what was right in the Lord's sight and walked in the ways of his ancestor David; he did not turn aside to the right or the left.

2 CHRONICLES 34:1-2

Memory Verse:

This is a verse you will want to commit to memory. Use the Scripture memory cards on page 95 for help.

"Trust in the Lord with all your heart, and do not rely on your own understanding; think about Him in all your ways, and He will guide you on the right paths." — Proverbs 3:5-6

Road Warrior:
Zach Hunter, Fighting Modern-Day Slavery

From migrant labor camps in Florida to brothels in Cambodia, slavery still exists. Between 600,000 and 800,000 people, mostly women and children, are trafficked across national borders while millions more are bought and sold within countries, according to the U.S. State Department.

Zach Hunter decided to do something about modern-day slavery. At the age of fifteen, he started a fund-raising campaign dubbed "Loose Change to Loosen Chains." The student-led campaign calls on youth to collect change and sell T-shirts to help abolish slavery.

"I really believe in my generation," Zach said of the effort. "A lot of kids are volunteering their own time on the weekends to help other people out. And that sort of gives me hope for my generation.

"In Isaiah 1:17, God says to learn to do right, seek justice, rescue your oppressed, defend orphans, and plead for the widow," Zach said. "It really doesn't get much more straightforward than that, I think. It's a biblical mandate to go out there and help those who are in need and who are oppressed. And that's really what the campaign is based on."

Zach also wrote *Be the Change: Your Guide to Freeing Slaves and Changing the World* and *Generation Change: Roll Up Your Sleeves and Change the World*, books published by Zondervan to help students understand the reality of slavery.

Zach encourages others to put themselves in the shoes of one of the twenty-seven million people currently enslaved and ask, "What if it were me?"[1]

What Influences You?

Have you ever noticed that when you and your friends want to grab a bite to eat, you typically end up going to the same place again and again? Can you remember the first time you went to a restaurant? Most of us can't. Yet the fast-food experience is a regular way of life for most of us.

What restaurants do you and your friends go to on a regular basis?

Why do you keep going back to the same place again and again?

mile marker
INFLUENCE: A power affecting a person, thing, or course of events; the power to sway or affect.

If you love a particular restaurant, then chances are someone or something influenced you to become a fan. There are many different influences that drive you one way or the other. Have you ever considered what "drives" you? Some people claim their parents or family members have the most influence in their lives, while others give their teachers, coaches, or friends credit for the direction they are headed.

Whether you realize it or not,

you've been influenced

—where you shop, what cell phone you have, the clothes you wear, and what's on your iPod.

Think of your preferences. Do you have a Fave 5?
Complete the chart below:

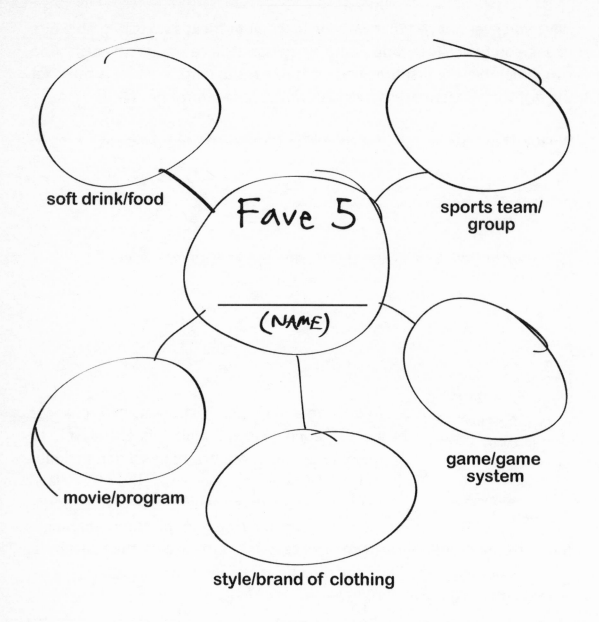

soft drink/food

Fave 5
_____
(NAME)

sports team/
group

game/game
system

movie/program

style/brand of clothing

travel tip

Friends can be more
influential than parents,
youth leaders, and
even God.
— Andy Stanley[2]

How did these become your favorites? What influenced your decisions? You are pushed and motivated by a wide variety of things — from people to social attitudes to your own feelings.

Think about the people and things that have influenced you in a positive or negative way. List the top three influences on your life in the blanks on the left. Then draw a line to indicate where it falls on the positive or negative gauge.

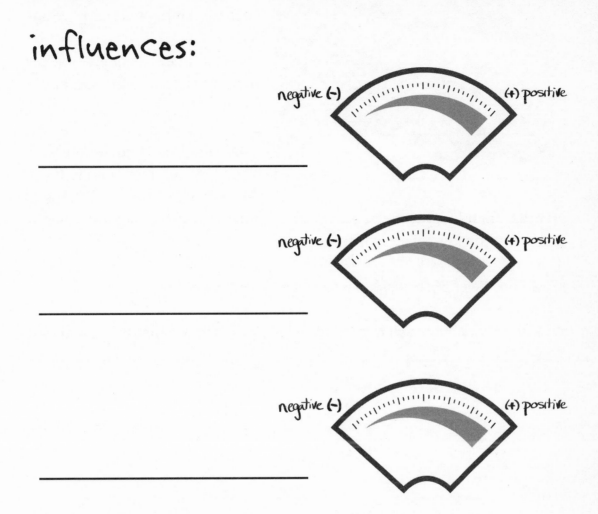

influences:

negative (–)   (+) positive

_____

negative (–)   (+) positive

_____

negative (–)   (+) positive

_____

You may be wondering why any of this matters. Here's the deal:

> The driving influence in your life will shape the person you become.

The Bible is full of stories about influential leaders. This study digs into the life of one of the most fascinating young leaders recorded in Scripture: Josiah. You'll learn some lessons from this guy who, in many ways, was just like you. You'll see how he and his friends completely changed the direction of their entire community and even nation!

travel tip
Sociologists tell us that even the most introverted individual will influence ten thousand other people during his or her lifetime! — John Maxwell[3]

Check the Rearview Mirror

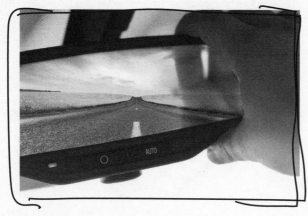

Read 2 Chronicles 34:1-2. Josiah became king at a very young age: eight.

How does an eight-year-old suddenly become the leader of a nation?

Josiah was born into the royal family. Unfortunately, it was a dysfunctional family. If you take a look at how his father and grandfather ruled, you will see a perfect picture of what *not* to do as a leader. Check out the following Scriptures.

☑ 2 Chronicles 33:1-10. Manasseh was Josiah's grandfather.

What words can you pull from Scripture to describe Manasseh's leadership style?

How would you characterize Manasseh as a leader? (Pick one.)

☐ **Everyone loved him, and he did great things for Jerusalem.**
☐ **He led Jerusalem away from God and did much evil.**
☐ **He was voted "most likely to be a good king."**
☐ **He was an evil leader.**
☐ **He was very concerned about the people of Jerusalem and how he led them.**

Josiah's grandfather was an evil leader who made God very angry. It gets worse. Josiah's father was Amon.

☑ Read 2 Chronicles 33:21-25 and answer the following questions about Amon. How old was Amon when he became king?

What kind of leader was Josiah's father?

How did Amon die?

At age eight, Josiah became king because his evil father was so awful that his own servants killed him. That's pretty bad.

Fortunately for Josiah, he had an ancestor who had set a much better example. Who is mentioned as part of Josiah's family tree in 2 Chronicles 34:2?

At a Crossroad

There are times along the journey when you come to a crossroad and have a chance to change direction.

Josiah had the opportunity to make a choice that would certainly define his destiny. He could choose to follow the example of his father and grandfather, or he could find another leader after which to model his life.

Josiah chose to return to the best example in his family history. His ancestor, King David, was described as a man after God's own heart.

Josiah was careful about the example he followed and the influences he allowed into his life. He recognized that some of the people around him did not provide the best influence.

Look at some choices Josiah made:

- **He didn't follow the example of his father.**
- **He didn't take his cues from his grandfather.**
- **He didn't choose to follow the traditions of the culture.**
- **He didn't worry about the approval of others.**
- **He didn't focus on being popular.**
- **He didn't follow the crowd.**
- **He didn't get sidetracked.**

Josiah chose to follow King David's example. He did what was right in God's eyes.

This decision had a huge impact on Josiah and the people in Jerusalem.

Every day you make decisions about what or who will influence you.

Some relationships and experiences will have a huge impact on your destiny while others won't.

Circle below the things you consider big decisions. Underline the ones you consider small decisions.

Who you date   Places you go
Where you go to church   How you dress
Friends you hang out with   Who you marry
Jobs you choose   Movies you watch
Whether or not to get pierced   College you attend

We make more big decisions than we realize! It would be nice if we were given some sort of sign that revealed which decisions will have a lasting impact on us. We need to make all our decisions as if they had the potential to impact us for a lifetime — because they might. Your everyday decisions need to be made with your destiny in mind.

☑ Read Proverbs 3:5-6.

What does it mean to "rely on your own understanding"?

Face it. Someone or something is currently shaping your view of life, your beliefs, your behaviors, your decisions, and your outlook. The question is:

Who or what will you allow to be your driving influence?

Off-Road Challenge

What influences your direction in life? Look up the verses below and ask God to speak to you as you read the following Scriptures. Write what Jesus said to do.

1. Matthew 4:18-22

2. Luke 5:27

3. Mark 1:17

   God didn't give Peter, Andrew, James, John, and Matthew a detailed road map to follow. He said, "Follow Me, I will show you."

What instructions did Jesus give in John 10:27?

☑ Read Romans 12:2; then answer the following questions.

What is the goal?
T _____

How does transformation happen?

Although renewing your mind may not mean much to you yet, compare it to loading your iPod, computer, or video system. When your system is loaded to the max and you want to add a new song, game, or program, you have to delete some of the old to make room for the new.

It's the same with your mind. You have been "loaded" with attitudes and thoughts that are contrary to Scripture. It's time to hit the erase button so the Word of God can take root in your heart and mind. Then transformation can occur.

Try this exercise to get a better handle on all of this.

☑ Write out Romans 12:2. In place of the phrase "conformed to this age," write "squeezed into the world's mold."

The best way to weaken cultural influence is to continually renew your mind. In doing so, you will yield more and more control of your life and decisions to the Holy Spirit.

> But the Counselor, the Holy Spirit — the Father will send Him in My name — will teach you all things and remind you of everything I have told you. (John 14:26)

Yield

What does "yield" mean to you? On the road, it means to slow down and let another vehicle go before you. Think about your life. What areas of your life are most yielded to the Holy Spirit? The Bible tells us to let the Spirit be in control and to be filled with the Spirit. Read Romans 8:5-9. Are you yielding to the Spirit or self?

What is one thing you will commit to yield to the Spirit today?

suggested tunes for the journey
Listen to "Lose Control" from the *We Can't Stand Sitting Down* album by Stellar Kart.

Straight Ahead

Once Josiah's decision to follow God was made, Scripture says he didn't turn to the right or left. He was not distracted by the "noise" around him. He was locked in on the target God set before him. He rose above circumstances — negative influences, obstacles, culture, and the crowd. Have you ever made a good decision only to cave in and change your mind when your friends made fun of you or when it got really hard to move forward? Most people have.

What kinds of things might influence you to turn right or left (be distracted) from the path of doing what's right in God's eyes?

In session 3 we will address distractions. For now, if Josiah had been more concerned about simply doing right in people's eyes, then he wouldn't have made the right choice.

When we give in and let the world influence our thoughts and actions not only do we choose to do what's right in the eyes of people instead of God, but we also fill our minds with teaching that goes against God's Word.

When was the last time you chose to do what was right in someone else's eyes instead of God's?

travel tip

In one of Jesus' most powerful times of teaching, He repeatedly said, "YOU HAVE HEARD IT SAID," and then He followed up by saying, "BUT I SAY . . ." This pattern shows that Jesus was intentionally naming certain worldly teachings that He wanted the people to unlearn and God-honoring principles He hoped they would learn (Matthew 5:21-44). — Richard Land

We all have been taught things that need to be addressed and challenged with the Word.

Imagine some of the things Josiah heard in his day. In spite of any advice to the contrary, he made the wise choice. Can you picture people lining up to give the young leader their opinions? (And you think your parents are preachy!) Josiah looked far and wide for a godly example to follow until his eyes landed on David. You also are surrounded by people who want to give you advice and opinions. Whether in person, in the media, or in the popular culture, the voices are loud!

Look below and circle which sources give you the most opinions and advice. You may also want to write in other sources.

church leader
friends   facebook
    parent   twitter
sister   myspace   music
    BFF   internet
    movies   tv

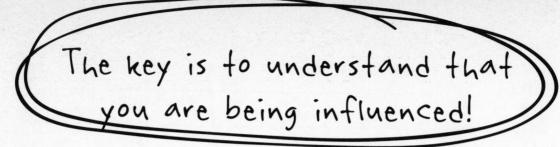

The key is to understand that you are being influenced!

Something or someone is driving you. When you resist the bad examples and follow the good examples, you — like Josiah — will make a difference.

Speed Bump

As we travel the road to destiny, prayer is critical. Use the following suggested prayer points as you communicate with God.

- ☐ Ask God to show you the dominant influences in your life.
- ☐ Praise God for the positive influences in your life.
- ☐ Ask God to teach you how to guard your heart and mind from influences that don't honor Him.
- ☐ Confess any influence you need to avoid. Pray for strength to do it.
- ☐ Ask God to help you make Him the dominant influence in your life.
- ☐ Thank God for speaking to you through this study.

What's the most significant statement or Scripture you read from session 1?

Be sure to review your memory verse: Proverbs 3:5-6

What does God want you to do in response to today's study?

Lessons from the Journey

This past summer I decided to try out for my high school football team. On the first day of practice, as we walked down to the practice field, it seemed like all of us, including the coaches, were sizing up the competition. There were guys who were six-foot-five, guys who could run fast, and others who had so much endurance they could run five miles and still not be tired.

Everyone out there had an obsession with winning. For better or worse, in the world of sports it is all about success and performance. But in the game of life, we can't always go undefeated.

God does not just look at our performance. Some things are more important to Him than how fast, how strong, or how tall I am; He is more interested in my heart and my relationship with Him.

Sometimes I get caught up in the race of pleasing my peers.

Unfortunately, that's often the way of the world. A person should not be judged by what he has or does not have.

There is a great example in the Bible: God told Samuel to go to the family of Jesse to find the new king. I imagine that some of Jesse's sons were great athletes, and some were the best hunters in Bethlehem, but the one God chose wasn't the fastest, the strongest, the one with the most awards, or the most popular guy in Bethlehem. God chose David because his heart was right with God. God chose David because of his heart and not his outward appearance (see 1 Samuel 16:7).

I need to remember to focus on my heart and not my performance.

—Luke Harper

Junior
Hendersonville, Tennessee

SESSION 2

THE CHASE IS ON:

How Far Will You Go?

"He did what was right in the LORD's sight and walked in the ways of his ancestor David; he did not turn aside to the right or the left. In the eighth year of his reign, while he was still a youth, Josiah began to seek the God of his ancestor David, and in the twelfth year he began to cleanse Judah and Jerusalem of the high places, the Asherah poles, the carved images, and the cast images."

2 CHRONICLES 34:2-3

Memory Verse:

Here is another verse that you will want to commit to memory. Use the Scripture memory cards on page 95 for help!

"But the Counselor, the Holy Spirit — the Father will send Him in My name — will teach you all things and remind you of everything I have told you." — John 14:26

Road Warrior:
Rebecca Stallard Inspired Others

An Illinois student's mission trip to Africa resulted in the collection of more than three hundred pairs of shoes for impoverished children in Zambia.

Their lack of what Americans see as basic necessities saddened ten-year-old Rebecca Stallard.

"I saw that I have so much, and they have so little," she wrote in an e-mail interview. "It made me very grateful for all I have here in the States. It has made me want less stuff, and to give them more."

Rebecca tells of a young Zambian boy who stood in line for two hours to get a pair of shoes, only to find there were no boys' shoes left.

He wanted shoes so badly that he went and stood in the girls' shoe line and picked out a pair of bright pink shoes. "That's how desperate he was for shoes," she said.

Rebecca's testimony convinced her friends to get involved in collecting shoes for these needy children.

"On their own initiative, the girls went to their school principal in November and asked if they could have a display at school for collecting shoes," a missions group leader at her church said.

They collected 318 pairs of new and gently worn children's shoes at school, and later opened collection sites at their church, a Christian bookstore, and a local discount store.

Their mission project taught the girls how God can use people of all ages to help others.[1]

The Chase Is On

Traveling along the road of life can be tricky anytime, but especially when you are moving at top speed. Do you ever feel like you are running too fast, doing all you can to just barely keep up? Students today are busier than ever before. From sports to school to friends to church to music to family to work — finding time for it all can be tough.

Make a list of everything you are involved in on a regular basis:

Circle the three things to which you devote the most time.

Living fast-paced lives makes it difficult to keep focus. Some people would say that we "chase" the things that interest us most. Think about it.

- If you are focused on making certain grades, you will *"chase"* a high GPA by studying and working hard in class.
- If you have your sights on a starting position on the team, you will *"chase"* that spot by working out and staying after practice to work with the coach.

- **If your dream is to be the next American Idol, you *"chase"* it by focusing on the music.**
- **If being labeled as cool is your goal, you *"chase"* that by keeping up with the latest fashion, cars, music, and so on.**

When Josiah was around your age, he made a crucial choice about what he would "chase" or seek.

☑ Read 2 Chronicles 34:2-3 and fill in the blanks.

In the eighth year of his reign, while he was still _____, Josiah began to seek _____.

How cool is that? It is not unusual to read in Scripture of how God uses young people. He sees value in us no matter our age. There is no guesswork involved here. Josiah was eight when he became king. Eight years into his reign he would be sixteen years old.

Josiah was young, like you, and the lessons from his life can apply to your life today. In the last session, we looked at influence and opinions. In this session we will examine where you place your focus and what things you seek.

What do you think it means to seek God?

mile marker
SEEKING:
Chasing after something with all your being.

When you seek something or someone, you are probably focused and determined to get what you are seeking. Right now you may say that you are seeking God, but are you really seeking Him?

If you are like most people, then you are pursuing everything but God. If He isn't your focus, you are looking for the wrong thing.

Compare your life to Josiah's. He was more concerned about "doing right in God's eyes" and "seeking Him" than anything else. What about you?

Which of these statements best describe your focus on God right now? (Check all that apply.)

- ☐ It is so foggy; I can't see a thing.
- ☐ Out of focus — not too many details.
- ☐ I can see clearly.
- ☐ I'm completely blinded by stuff.
- ☐ I'm waiting for daylight.
- ☐ I see other people who can see perfectly.
- ☐ Other: _____
- ☐ Other: _____
- ☐ Other: _____

mile marker
LOOKING:
Directing one's gaze toward someone or something.

The Reward Is Yours

Remember the difference between looking and seeking?

It's about intensity and focus. When you can see the potential value in something, you are more likely to chase after it or pursue it.

Now for the good news: When you follow Josiah's example and seek after God, guess what happens? Rewards. Check it out for yourself.

mile marker
CHASE:
To pursue in order to catch up with.

☑ Read the following verses and list what happens when you seek God.

Hebrews 11:6

James 4:8

Proverbs 8:17

Matthew 6:33

Jeremiah 29:13

As a child, you probably played hide-and-seek. Did you ever get frustrated because you couldn't find someone? That will never happen with the Lord. The incredible thing is that the God who spoke the world into existence wants you to seek Him. He promises that when you seek Him, you will find Him. He wants to be actively involved in your life. He wants to be your guide. He will never steer you in the wrong direction.

travel tip

God will never back down on a promise, so you can be sure that when you find a promise in the Bible, it is rock solid.
— Richard Land

Off-Road Challenge

Jesus was a seeker!

☑ Read the following Scriptures; then list some of the places that Jesus went to seek God.[2] Notice the time Jesus would seek God.

Luke 5:16

Luke 6:12

Luke 22:39-41

Mark 1:35

Mark 6:46-47

Jesus sought after God all the time — early in the morning, during the day, at night, and sometimes all night. He frequently found places to hide away where He could be alone with His Father. At other times, He would seek God with people around Him.

travel tip
Seeking God in prayer — "a relationship with the Heavenly Father, Lord and Master, in which you speak to God and He speaks to you and guides you."
— Claude King[3]

- **Jesus sought God when He was putting His team together (see Luke 6:12-16).**
- **Jesus sought God about where He should preach and teach (see Mark 1:35-39).**
- **Jesus sought God on what He should preach and teach (see John 12:49).**
- **Jesus sought God before His arrest in the garden (see Luke 22:39-41,47-54).**

What does seeking God and finding Him have to do with your life at school, on the team, in your family, or in your job? Consider it this way: Jesus gave us an example to follow, so we must give serious attention to how He lived His life. If Jesus, the Son of God, needed to be alone and seek direction from His Father, don't you think we need to do the same?[4]

travel tip
You will grow closer to God when you spend focused time with Him!
— Jay Strack

Where you go for help or advice usually depends on the need or issue. But what if you knew for sure that you could go to one place or one person and have every one   of your needs met — would you go? Of course you would; who wouldn't!

Yield

☑ Read Matthew 6:33. Do you see the promise in this verse? If you seek God first, then He will meet all your other needs. ("All these things will be provided for you.") The problem comes when we try to handle our issues and needs on our own.

☑ Review Proverbs 3:5-6 from the previous session. What do these verses say is the opposite of trusting the Lord with all your heart?

You have probably noticed that leaning on your own understanding is about reacting and doing what you want to do without considering what God's Word has to say. So many people are tempted to "check in" with God at times when it is convenient for them and forget about Him the rest of the time.

If the teacher in your toughest class gives an open-book test, would you refuse to use the book and instead go with what you know? If she offered to help you with any questions that you could not answer, would you refuse her help? No way.

Yet that's exactly what happens spiritually when you don't seek and trust in the Lord and instead rely on your own understanding. In what areas of your life do you place more confidence in yourself than in God?

Stay Focused

Drivers must keep their eyes on the road and stay focused in order to avoid accidents and get to their destination safely. When your focus gets misplaced, bad things can happen. On this road to destiny, you may have been seeking God and living like Josiah when suddenly your attention was diverted to the point that you lost your way. You may like the idea of seeking God but realize you are so busy chasing other things that you have no time left for Him.

suggested tunes for the journey
Listen to "Never Going Back to OK" from the album *Never Going Back to OK* by The Afters.

Label this drawing with your name and then draw some eyes. List the things you are seeking, or focusing on, in front of your eyes. You can draw pictures to represent them or make a list.

It's important to realize that the things you have listed may not be bad things. It is possible they are good things that need to be a part of your life. The problem comes when those people or things take God's place in your life. The Bible has a word for that: IDOLATRY.

Write the definition for "idol":

How could we possibly think that anything or anyone could substitute for the Almighty God of the universe?

At some point, we have all done exactly that. The key is to recognize when your focus is off and to turn back toward seeking God.

Josiah made the choice to seek God while he was young. Have you made that same choice? Lots of your friends think they will put off that decision until they are older. What if King Josiah had thought that way? If he had waited to follow God, what would have happened? What would have happened to his people? Who knows?

None of us are guaranteed tomorrow. None of us knows how long our lives will be. If Josiah had waited to seek God, he might have run out of time. You might too.

List five reasons why you should seek God.

1.

2.

3.

4.

5.

Today's the day —
your destiny will be affected
by the choice you make.

When, Where, and How Do You Seek God?[5]

STUDENT	WHO	WHEN	WHERE	WHAT
Emma, 9th Grade, Plano, TX	My sister and I	We get up early every morning	Kitchen table	We go through a devotional book
Brayden, 7th Grade, Calhoun, GA	By myself	Before I go to bed at night and sometimes during the day	My room or on the back deck	P.R.A.Y. (Pray, Repent, Ask, Yield)
Seth, 12th Grade, Charlotte, NC	My best friend, Travis	Every Wednesday at 4:00 p.m.	Starbucks or the park	We study a character in the Bible; right now: "Joseph"
Paige, 11th Grade, Jackson, MS	Group of friends	Every Thursday night	A friend's house	We go through a Bible study; right now: Beth Moore's on Esther

↖ (this space is yours)

What's the most significant statement or Scripture you read from session 2?

What does God want you to do in response to today's study?

Review Your Memory Verses

Review your memory verses from sessions 1 and 2. Work on them and then find a friend and recite each verse.

SESSION 1 ▷

"Trust in the LORD with all your heart, and do not rely on your own understanding; think about Him in all your ways, and He will guide you on the right paths." — Proverbs 3:5-6

SESSION 2 ▷

"But the Counselor, the Holy Spirit — the Father will send Him in My name — will teach you all things and remind you of everything I have told you." — John 14:26

Speed Bump

The road to leadership requires prayer. Josiah's life provides a glimpse of someone who had a true relationship with his heavenly Father. Josiah wasn't just religious; Josiah sought God! Consider the following as you seek God this week:

- ☐ **Find a place to hide and seek God.**
- ☐ **Spend at least thirty minutes seeking God.**
- ☐ **Write a letter to God.**
- ☐ **Keep a conversation going with God throughout your day.**
- ☐ **Find a friend and ask if he or she would like to meet and seek God with you.**

NOTES

Lessons from the Journey

When I was little, my favorite game to play was hide-and-seek. I could fit in those hiding spots that people wouldn't even think to look at! If I wasn't found, I would get tired of waiting and come out. Sometimes I would make funny sounds to try to be found after what seemed like an eternity of waiting!

There are two roles in the game of hide-and-seek: the hider and the seeker. As followers of Christ, we are supposed to do both — hide from distractions and seek God!

Psalm 32 proclaims the greatness of finding God. David declares the Lord is his "hiding place" and that God surrounded him with "joyful shouts of deliverance." God has promised us that we can also find Him! In 1 Chronicles 28:9, David tells his son Solomon, "If you seek Him, He will be found by you."

For many followers of Christ, "hiding and seeking" might sound like a "quiet time." Yet in Psalm 32, David proclaimed how God surrounded him with "joyful shouts of deliverance"! That doesn't sound very quiet to me. Later in verse 11 David even says, "Shout for joy."

My love for "hiding and seeking" has changed somewhat. Now the more I hide and seek, the more intimate I get with the Lord. And the more intimate I get with Him, the easier it gets to live in Him and not in my flesh!

—Jody Johnston

Senior
Covington, Louisiana

SESSION 3

ROADBLOCK:

What's Standing in Your Way?

In the eighth year of his reign, while he was still a youth, Josiah began to seek the God of his ancestor David, and in the twelfth year he began to cleanse Judah and Jerusalem of the high places, the Asherah poles, the carved images, and the cast images. Then in his presence the altars of the Baals were torn down, and the incense altars that were above them he chopped down. The Asherah poles, the carved images, and the cast images he shattered, crushed to dust, and scattered over the graves of those who had sacrificed to them. He burned the bones of the priests on their altars. So he cleansed Judah and Jerusalem. [He did the same] in the cities of Manasseh, Ephraim, and Simeon, and as far as Naphtali [and] on their surrounding mountain shrines. He tore down the altars, and he smashed the Asherah poles and the carved images to powder. He chopped down all the incense altars throughout the land of Israel and returned to Jerusalem.

2 CHRONICLES 34:3-7

Memory Verse:

This one's important!

"Search me, God, and know my heart; test me and know my concerns. See if there is any offensive way in me; lead me in the everlasting way." — Psalm 139:23-24

Road Warrior:
Nate Richards, Taking a Stand

Nate Richards was tired of seeing his football teammates damaging themselves and the team by engaging in dangerous behavior. Specifically, Nate was tired of the drug and alcohol use among the group on the weekends. Though not rampant, it was definitely an issue.

Nate, a high school senior in Texas, decided to act. He called a team meeting the day before two-a-day practices began. Flanked by a couple of teammates, Nate addressed the players about the problems he saw.

"I thought that during the season, they shouldn't be doing that," Nate said about the drinking and drug use. "It not only hurts the team, it hurts them." He said his decision to stand up for morality was fueled by his Christian faith.

Nate, the team's center, asked each player to commit to abstaining from alcohol and drug use over the course of the season. He hoped that commitment would develop habits in his teammates that would last even longer. The team endorsed Nate's proposal and established the punishment for those breaking the new rules.

"Avoiding drugs and alcohol is something we [confront] as a coaching staff on a daily basis," said Kevin Atkinson, the team's coach. "The most important thing for young people to realize is that being a leader isn't a popularity contest. You can't be afraid to do the right thing. When you're a leader, it's lonely at the top."

Nate took a risk by confronting his teammates, Atkinson said, but in the process has shown what true leadership is all about.

Dangerous Blind Spots

New drivers are constantly warned about blind spots — those areas around your vehicle that are hard to see from the driver's seat.

Mirrors help, but blind spots are dangerous. Even when you are focused in the right direction and heading down the road, you must remember to check all around you to make sure nothing is creeping up that could distract your focus.

It is not unusual for someone to be following after God and seeking Him, and then have their attention or focus diverted to something else — a new love interest, a different group of friends, a band, a new hobby, a new sport.

Things can creep in and steal your attention away from where it needs to be. Josiah was king. He could have been distracted by many things — his wealth and power far exceeded anything we know — but he sought God.

travel tip
Leaders do not allow themselves to be distracted from their God-given purpose.
— Richard Land[1]

In what areas of life are you most likely to be distracted? Circle all that apply.

School   Athletics   Other:

Free Time   Dating   _____

Entertainment Home   _____

Work   Music   _____

Since Josiah was king, he likely had more things to distract him than you do.

What are the things in your blind spot that may be sneaking up on you? List them on the car.

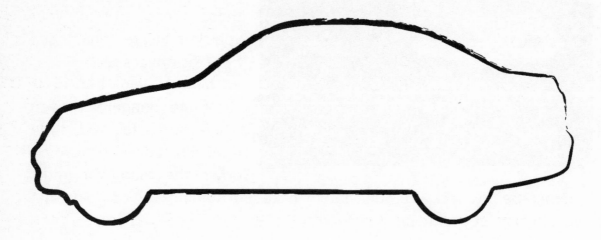

In the previous session we focused on how Josiah began to seek God at a young age. After Josiah's heart changed toward the things of the Lord, his actions began to change too.

☑ Read 2 Chronicles 34:3-7.

Wow! <u>This guy was pretty radical</u> in his next steps. Sometimes the journey can be full of roadblocks or things that will hinder our progress. Josiah completely cleared his path! Scripture uses "shattered," "crushed to dust," and "scattered" to describe this process.

The things his father and grandfather allowed and encouraged were no longer acceptable. He made major changes as king. It was a new day!

mile marker
ROADBLOCK:
A barrier on a road to stop traffic.

☑ Read 2 Chronicles 34:3-7 and circle every time Josiah's name appears and every time you see a "he" that refers to the king.

In the eighth year of his reign, while he was still a youth, Josiah began to seek the God of his ancestor David, and in the twelfth year he began to cleanse Judah and Jerusalem of the high places, the Asherah poles, the carved images, and the cast images. Then in his presence the altars of the

Baals were torn down, and the incense altars that were above them he chopped down. The Asherah poles, the carved images, and the cast images he shattered, crushed to dust, and scattered over the graves of those who had sacrificed to them. He burned the bones of the priests on their altars. So he cleansed Judah and Jerusalem. [He did the same] in the cities of Manasseh, Ephraim, and Simeon, and as far as Naphtali [and] on their surrounding mountain shrines. He tore down the altars, and he smashed the Asherah poles and the carved images to powder. He chopped down all the incense altars throughout the land of Israel and returned to Jerusalem.

How many references to Josiah did you find?

What does your discovery tell you about Josiah's commitment to cleaning up the land?

   The use of "he" indicates that Josiah was personally involved in the effort. He didn't sit back and command others to do the dirty work. He didn't assume others would do it. He took the time to oversee the cleanup. He flushed everything that got in the way of worshipping God.

Deal with It

When Josiah made the decision to seek God, his heart changed. Things that had always been part of his life were no longer okay. He examined his ways and the ways of his people and was willing to do what it took to bring the focus back to God.

☑ Read verses 3 and 4 again. Circle the specific idols Josiah destroyed in order to cleanse the land.

In the eighth year of his reign, while he was still a youth, Josiah began to seek the God of his ancestor David, and in the twelfth year he began to cleanse Judah and Jerusalem of the high places, the Asherah poles, the carved images, and the cast images. Then in his presence the altars of the Baals were torn down, and the incense altars that were above them he chopped down. The Asherah poles, the carved images, and the cast images he shattered, crushed to dust, and scattered over the graves of those who had sacrificed to them.

Do you know what these things were and why it was a big deal that Josiah got rid of them? Each of these specific items represented a form of worship to something other than God. Throughout Israel's history, God had warned the people about what would happen if they allowed these types of influences to penetrate their culture. Yet the people continually turned to their idols instead of the Lord. Does any of this sound familiar?

> *travel tip*
> Throughout history God's people have tended to turn to substitutes for their relationship with Him.
> — Henry Blackaby and Claude King[2]

You probably don't have an Asherah pole in your house or an altar of Baal in the backyard, but you may have allowed some forms of idolatry to creep into your life. Remember, anything that takes God's place is an idol.

☑ Look at the idols you circled and think of some modern-day things that might represent idolatry.

When you see the actions that Josiah took, one thing is obvious: This young man was passionate about his relationship with God. Josiah yielded his life to God, and that led to some big changes. He didn't change his behavior to fit a certain mold; he yielded and surrendered his life. Josiah changed from the inside out.

You may need to get rid of some idols of the heart, tear down some strongholds, and remove yourself from tempting situations. Ask God to guide you through this process. Use David's prayer recorded in Psalm 51 as a guide.

Road Map for Success

At times the things that need to be cleaned out are your personal choices. Sometimes a history of ungodly or negative choices exists in your life or in your family that needs to be stopped and addressed.

Josiah's family was royal — a royal mess.

When he became king, Josiah had the opportunity to make necessary changes. Although you have no control over some things that have happened in your family, you do have the choice to break the cycle of negative and ungodly behaviors. Like Josiah, you are personally accountable to God.

☑ Check out this list of behaviors that can be handed down through generations. Mark the ones people in your family have experienced.

- ☐ Alcoholism
- ☐ Drug abuse
- ☐ Divorce
- ☐ Bitterness
- ☐ Adultery
- ☐ Premarital sex
- ☐ Lying

- ☐ Physical abuse
- ☐ Materialism
- ☐ Verbal abuse
- ☐ Suicide
- ☐ Obesity
- ☐ Eating disorders
- ☐ Other: _____

All sorts of things are accepted as normal behaviors simply because they have been passed along through families for years. Yet we have the responsibility to evaluate whether or not certain activities and actions are part of God's plan for our lives.

Whether inherited from family members or influenced by the culture we live in, what negative patterns do you want to break free from in your life?

How can you follow Josiah's example of breaking the cycle? One idea is to have a road map or plan of action to get you from where you are to where God wants you to be. Determine early on what can help keep you safe from destructive choices and distractions that will inevitably come your way.

Along the road, you will see signs warning you of possible dangers.

To help protect yourself spiritually and break the cycle of negative behavior, write your own warning signs in the space provided.

beware of friends who make poor choices

It's good to plan ahead, but remember that you can't do any of these things on your own. Josiah was seeking God. Every good thing he did was through the power and strength of Almighty God. That power is exactly what you need too.

Off-Road Challenge

Let's look at what Jesus asks of His followers.

☑ Read Luke 9:23-24 and then fill in the missing words. Jesus mentions three things you must do to follow Him.

"If anyone wants to come with Me, he must _____ himself, take up his _____ daily, and _____ Me."

Jesus asked His followers to deny themselves, take up their cross daily, and follow Him.

Self-centeredness is one of the main things that gets in the way of being a follower of Christ. Sometimes we get the idea that we have a better plan for our lives than God does. You want to do life on your own. You want to call the shots. You want to be in the driver's seat.[3]

What does it mean to deny yourself?

mile marker
Taking up the cross refers to the willingness to endure persecution, rejection, reproach, shame, suffering, and even martyrdom for the sake of Christ.
— John MacArthur[4]

Yield

Is it about time to clean out your life? <u>Are there some things you need to flush?</u> To help identify these things, ask yourself: "What is standing in the way of my relationship with Christ?" Have you given your passions or priorities to anyone or anything other than God?

☑ Read Psalm 139:23-24. Use it as your prayer. These verses will help you open your life up to examination and see what needs to be cleaned out. Regularly praying that God will show you what needs to go is a valuable practice.

When a person acknowledges their sinfulness and seeks to follow Jesus, He expects them to take personal responsibility for their sin and confess it to God. To repent means to go in a different direction — to turn away from living life your way, and to choose to make Him Lord. You decide to live His way, according to His will.[5]

Use this scale to mark the degree to which you are yielded to God. What can you do to more fully surrender control to the Holy Spirit?

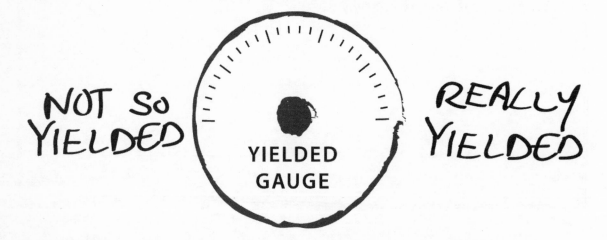

NOT SO YIELDED

YIELDED GAUGE

REALLY YIELDED

How will your life be different if you choose to yield more fully?

When you take a stand for Christ and live your life as a passionate follower of Jesus, you will be noticed. Josiah was willing to stand out and be different as king. The people may not have been happy about all the changes he made, but he followed through and did the right thing — the tough thing. When you stand up for God, you stand out. So be prepared.

If someone watched you this past week, what would they say about your relationship with Jesus Christ?

- ☐ **Definitely a Christ follower.**
- ☐ **No way is that person a Christian.**
- ☐ **Maybe (but maybe not).**
- ☐ **If that's what a Christian is, then no thanks.**
- ☐ **Whatever he or she has, I want it too.**
- ☐ **He or she lives just like everyone else.**
- ☐ **Acts one way at church and totally different other places.**

Speed Bump

The road to leadership requires prayer. Josiah made the decision to seek God, examine His ways and the ways of His people, and do whatever it took to bring the focus back to God.

- ☐ **Thank God for what He has revealed to you in this session.**
- ☐ **Ask God to show you what is standing in the way of your relationship with Him.**
- ☐ **Ask God to show you any substitute you have put in place of Him.**
- ☐ **Ask God to show you ways you have departed from Him for someone or something else.**
- ☐ **Ask God to change you to be more like Him. Ask God to help you be less self-focused and more God-focused.**
- ☐ **Tell God the kind of relationship you would like to have with Him.**
- ☐ **Tell God you are willing to surrender to His will.**

Be sure to review your memory verse: Psalm 129:23-24

Lessons from the Journey

I love Saturdays. It may be the sleeping in or watching ESPN uninterrupted. But there is one phrase that ruins it all: "TIME TO CLEAN YOUR ROOM."

In my haste to get back to *SportsCenter*, I search for the easiest way to remove all the stuff that litters my room.

As I scan my room for a place to cram everything, I take the most amazing escape route to ESPN — my closet. I cram every single thing inside my closet and somehow manage to keep the door from flying open. When Mom comes in for inspection, I'm praying she doesn't open the closet.

You see, when my mom stands in the doorway of my room, it looks really clean. Thankfully she doesn't open my closet or look under the bed.

Sometimes my room resembles my heart. It may look clean, but if you were able to thoroughly search my heart, I would be embarrassed.

Isn't that how life is sometimes? I run in and clean up my life before people get a good look at me. I put on this "clean room look" before people when really I have hidden things in my life that are messy.

The only way I can truly be content is if I let God clean my heart and help me to not hide my sins in the "closet." Whenever I open the doors of my heart and give God total access, He is always faithful to clean up my mess.

—Luke Harper

Junior
Hendersonville, Tennessee

SESSION 4

GPS:

How Are You Going to Get There?

When they brought out the money that had been deposited in the LORD's temple, Hilkiah the priest found the book of the law of the LORD [written] by the hand of Moses. Consequently, Hilkiah told Shaphan the court secretary, "I have found the book of the law in the LORD's temple," and he gave the book to Shaphan. Shaphan took the book to the king, and also reported, "Your servants are doing all that was placed in their hands. They have emptied out the money that was found in the LORD's temple and have put it into the hand of the overseers and the hand of those doing the work." Then Shaphan the court secretary told the king, "Hilkiah the priest gave me a book," and Shaphan read it in the presence of the king. When the king heard the words of the law, he tore his clothes. Then he commanded Hilkiah, Ahikam son of Shaphan, Abdon son of Micah, Shaphan the court secretary, and the king's servant Asaiah, "Go. Inquire of the LORD for me and for those remaining in Israel and Judah, concerning the words of the book that was found. For great is the LORD's wrath that is poured out on us because our fathers have not kept the word of the LORD in order to do everything written in this book."

2 CHRONICLES 34:14-21

Memory Verse:

Don't forget to commit this verse to memory.

"For the word of God is living and effective and sharper than any two-edged sword, penetrating as far as to divide soul, spirit, joints, and marrow; it is a judge of the ideas and thoughts of the heart." — Hebrews 4:12

Road Warriors:
Alex and Brett Harris, The New American Rebelution

Alabama State Supreme Court interns. Statewide grassroots campaign directors. Website designers and bloggers. Published authors. Conference speakers. These are just a few titles nineteen-year-olds Alex and Brett Harris could have on their resumes.

These twin brothers from Portland, Oregon, are in many ways just normal teenagers. They love filmmaking, music, basketball, soccer, and food. But in some ways they aren't quite average teenagers. They started "The Rebelution"—a "teenage rebellion against the low expectations of an ungodly culture" that began in August 2005.

According to these contemporary revolutionaries, today's society associates negativity and trouble with teens, and "allows, encourages, and even trains young people to remain childish for much longer than necessary." They believe the "media-saturated youth culture is constantly reinforcing lower and lower standards and expectations."

The Harris brothers say the best years in many teenagers' lives are wasted; they never get the chance to reach their God-given potential.

"We live in a culture that wants to tell us how to act, how to think, how to look, and how to talk. It tells us what to wear, what to buy, and where to buy it. It tells us what to dream, what to value, and what to live for — and it's not Christ."

These two brothers hope to challenge young people to join The Rebelution, refuse to be defined by our culture, reject the lies and corruption of the media, and return to biblical and historical levels of character, competence, and collaboration.[1]

Need Directions?

Being lost is never fun. We've all been there at some point. (It's okay to admit it, guys.) Have you ever tried to find a place without having directions? It's frustrating. Sometimes all you need is a marker to make the right turn on the right road. At other times the directions are so complicated and there are so many opportunities for wrong turns that the safest route is to follow someone who knows the way.

Describe a time when you were lost. How did it make you feel?

A GPS is a great addition to any vehicle. Most people like to know where they are, where they are going, and how to get there. That's why a GPS is popular. It seems like a foolproof plan. The little gadget talks with a satellite and then relays information back and forth. But there can be problems.

It's actually possible to have a working GPS and end up in the wrong place. How? If you program the device with bad information, like the wrong zip code, you could drive off into a lake!

It's important to provide accurate information so you can trust the GPS to steer you on the right path.

Think about the influences you have allowed to direct your life. Where has your focus been lately? Have you managed to stay on the right path, or are you simply wandering around?

In this study of Josiah, we have touched on several things to help you stay on track in your quest to define your destiny God's way. Now it's time to investigate the role the Word of God played in the life of Josiah's people and what it should mean in your life.

> *mile marker*
> **BOOK OF THE LAW:** A collection of writings by Moses that had been inspired by God. The first five books in our Bible (the Pentateuch).

☑ Read 2 Chronicles 34:14-15.

What did Hilkiah, the priest, find?

Where had it been?

Do you know where your Bible is? Have you ever lost your Bible? Trying to remember if your Bible is by your bed or in the car is nothing compared to what happened in the temple that day.

The Word of God had been lost for something like seventy-five years. There weren't other copies in people's homes or in the hotels where they stayed. It had been lost and apparently forgotten. When the Word of God is "lost," bad things happen.

Keep in mind that the temple had not been used to worship God for a while. Imagine being a priest following the king's instructions to clean the temple and stumbling on a lost copy of the Scripture.

You would expect that of all the people, the priest would have known where it was.

But that is another indication of the spiritual condition of this community. The people had become so evil that even the priest had forgotten the Word of God. That's bad!

It is one thing for *you* to lose your Bible, but you would probably have a big problem if *your pastor* lost his Bible and failed to do anything about it for years and years. In Josiah's day, the Word had been neglected for so long that all the copies had deteriorated or been destroyed.

If your Bible disappeared, how long would it take for you to miss it?

What are some ways that you neglect the Word of God today?

Compare the negative impact on Josiah's people with what might happen to you if you continue neglecting the Word of God. What are some possible consequences?

Just as a GPS must be programmed accurately and with good information, your life needs to be filled with the truth of the Word. Your response to the Word should be like Josiah's. Look at what happened when the king learned of the priest's discovery.

Instant Reaction

☑ Read 2 Chronicles 34:16-19. The worker went to Josiah to report what had happened that day in their work. In the course of telling him of the progress, he mentioned that the priest found a book. He read from it as Josiah listened.

What did Josiah do when he heard the reading?

How quickly did Josiah respond?

What are some possible reasons Josiah reacted so strongly?

- ☐ He was scared.
- ☐ He was excited.
- ☐ He was convicted.
- ☐ He recognized it as Scripture.

Any one of these (and probably all of them) is a correct answer. When Josiah heard the Word, he recognized it as Scripture. He realized that he and those before him had sinned greatly against the Lord. He felt convicted and immediately responded by tearing his clothing. This was a sign of great distress and emotion. When was the last time you were convicted by hearing the Word?

How does the Word of God affect you? (Check all that apply.)

- ☐ Makes me feel good
- ☐ Shows me my sin
- ☐ Doesn't affect me at all
- ☐ Bores me
- ☐ Makes me care a little bit
- ☐ Confuses me
- ☐ Strengthens me
- ☐ Encourages me

How can reading or not reading God's Word influence the way you live your life?

Off-Road Challenge

Second Timothy 3:16-17 describes the power of the Word in our lives.

☑ Read these verses. Check any of the things below that apply to Scripture.

☐ **Inspired by God**   ☐ **Divinely inspired**
☐ **Breathed out by God**   ☐ **Given by inspiration of God**
☐ **God breathed**

(Your answer may vary depending on your translation of the Bible.)

According to verse 16, all Scripture comes from the mouth of God. When you read your Bible, you hear God speak.

What are four things Scripture is useful or profitable for?

1. _____
   _____

2. _____
   _____

3. _____
   _____

4. _____
   _____

According to verse 17, Scripture is helpful to us when we read it and apply it to our lives. Read verse 17 again. What will Scripture accomplish in your life?

How we respond to God's Word typically depends on what is happening in our lives. *The important thing is that we do respond.*

That day for Josiah was a spiritual marker. It was a time he could look back on, recognizing that from that day forward, he was never the same again. Think about some spiritual markers you have experienced. The day a person places his or her faith in Jesus Christ is certainly one of those days.

What are some of your spiritual markers?

mile marker

A spiritual marker identifies a time of transition, decision or direction when you clearly know God has guided you.
— Henry Blackaby and Claude King[2]

Yield

One way to think of the Bible's influence on our lives is to look at it like a mirror. When you look in a mirror, you see your image. If you have a big pimple on your forehead, you see it and deal with it.

When you look into the perfect Word of God, it will reflect or reveal the imperfections in your life.

James 1:23-24 says, "If anyone is a hearer of the word and not a doer, he is like a man looking at his own face in a mirror; for he looks at himself, goes away, and right away forgets what kind of man he was."

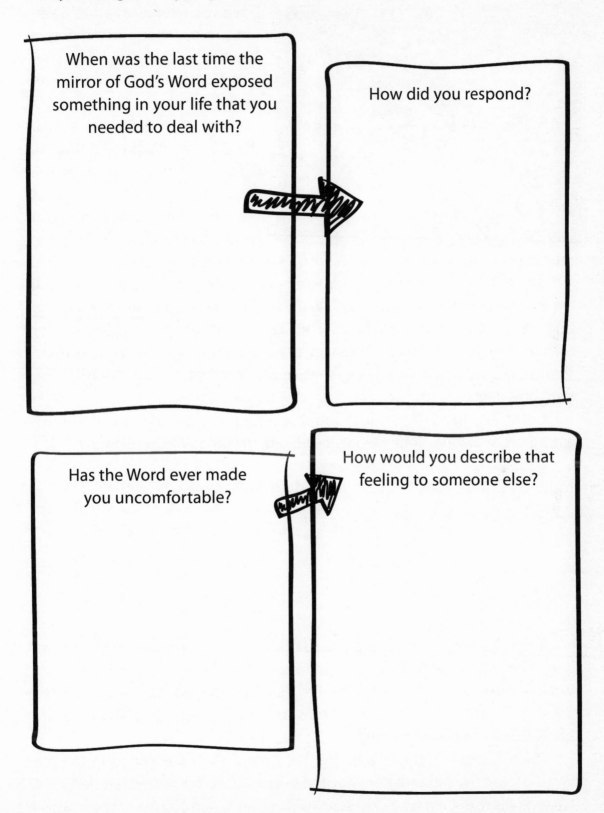

When was the last time the mirror of God's Word exposed something in your life that you needed to deal with?

How did you respond?

Has the Word ever made you uncomfortable?

How would you describe that feeling to someone else?

Following the Right Direction

Have you ever listened to a sermon and thought someone must have called the preacher and told him what was going on in your life?

That is an example of how the Bible is alive and personal. Odds are that no one called the preacher. No matter what was taught from Scripture, you would have received the same message. That's how conviction works. It's a great illustration of these verses.

Whatever sin needs to be addressed in your life is the one the Word will confront. Many people who don't want to change are <u>uncomfortable and edgy</u> when they go to church. They will do everything they can to avoid or escape the discomfort that comes with conviction of sin. Sadly, they keep themselves from the very thing that can relieve them from the resulting guilt and pain.

Living like Josiah is not just about reacting to the Word. It's also about acting on the Word. Notice what Josiah did after the Word was found.

☑ Read 2 Chronicles 34:20-21. What did Josiah do next?

It is important that we respond to the Bible in the right manner. But we also must allow the teachings of Scripture to shape how we live our lives. We must put into practice the things that God is teaching us. One of the amazing things about Josiah is how quickly he responded — Scripture became his navigational tool.[3]

Keep in mind that this was the first time Josiah had encountered the Word of God. He immediately wanted to have a better understanding of it. He took his standing with God seriously.

Josiah was desperate for more of the Word. When was the last time you cared about God's Word so much that you were desperate for it?

Is God's Word an active part of your life? How often do you use God's Word?

Where do you fall on the gauge as you think about your passion for God's Word? Draw a line to indicate where you fall on the gauge.

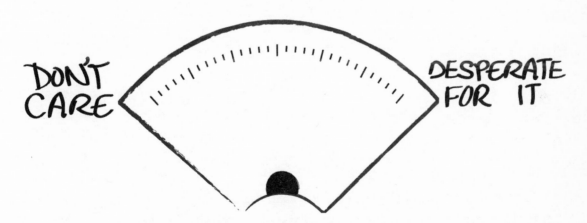

How does a person who has had their sins forgiven, been redeemed, and is now promised heaven instead of hell come to the point that God's Word is no big deal? It can and does happen to many people. You can have the Word in your life without any personal meaning. Unless you use the Word as your navigational tool for daily life, you are not following the right directions.

Just like a GPS, once you pull up a map, you can lose the signal from the satellite. The map remains on your screen, but no fresh information is displayed.

In your spiritual life this is called "going through the motions." It happens when your connection with God is neglected or "dropped" with nothing fresh coming in.

Have you ever felt like your spiritual "batteries" were running low? How do you think you get to that point?

Once you are saved, you *cannot* lose your relationship with Christ. However, it's possible, and all too common, for believers to live their daily lives without the power of the Holy Spirit. It happened to the people in Josiah's day, and it will happen to you if you don't make plans to prevent it.

Remember some of the reasons the people "lost" the Word so that you can avoid falling into the same pit.

travel tip
Just as a baby has to have milk to sustain its life physically, you have to have the Scripture to sustain your life spiritually.
— Howard Hendricks[4]

They were uncaring and unconcerned about the things of God. They had allowed all kinds of idols to creep into their lives. They lost their focus on what was right in God's eyes.

Josiah resisted the culture and stood for God. You can too. Commit now to being focused in the right direction, continually connected to God, and desperate for a fresh work of the Spirit in your life. You have the perfect tool for navigating your life. Use it.

At a Crossroad

What are the signs in your life that indicate your relationship with Christ is in a rut or that you are just going through the motions?

☐ **Do you check in at church and expect your attendance to get you through the week?**
☐ **Are you pursuing a daily relationship with God through prayer and Bible study?**
☐ **Do you regularly confess your sin and repent?**

Stop now and pray through the things God is showing you about your passion for Him.

What's the most significant statement or Scripture you read from session 4?

What does God want you to do in response to today's study?

travel tip

1. Text a Bible verse to a friend with a note that you are praying for him or her.
2. Read God's Word, record God's Word, and reflect on God's Word.
3. Journal. Write down a verse in a notebook and then rewrite it in your own words.
4. Find a prayer in the Bible and pray that Scripture to God. (See Colossians 1:9-10.)
5. Read Scripture aloud to a family member.
6. Write Scriptures on note cards and place them in your locker, car, on the bathroom mirror, or on the kitchen table.
7. Memorize one Scripture passage a month.
8. Pray before you read your Bible. Ask God to reveal Himself and His Truth to you.
9. Do a character study on a person in the Bible.
10. Look up a verse in an online Bible and meditate on that verse. (See Joshua 1:8.)[5]

Review Your Memory Verses

Review your Scripture memory verses from sessions 1 through 4. Then find a friend and recite each verse.

SESSION 1 ▷

"Trust in the LORD with all your heart, and do not rely on your own understanding; think about Him in all your ways, and He will guide you on the right paths." — Proverbs 3:5-6

SESSION 2 ▷

"But the Counselor, the Holy Spirit — the Father will send Him in My name — will teach you all things and remind you of everything I have told you." — John 14:26

SESSION 3 ▷

"Search me, God, and know my heart; test me and know my concerns. See if there is any offensive way in me; lead me in the everlasting way." — Psalm 139:23-24

SESSION 4 ▷

"For the word of God is living and effective and sharper than any two-edged sword, penetrating as far as to divide soul, spirit, joints, and marrow; it is a judge of the ideas and thoughts of the heart." — Hebrews 4:12

Speed Bump

The road to leadership requires prayer. Josiah responded quickly when he heard the Word of God. From that point on, Scripture became his life navigational tool.

- [ ] Thank God for what He has revealed to you in this session.
- [ ] Ask Him to show you how He would like you to respond to Him in light of what you just learned.
- [ ] Ask God to speak to you and help you understand His Word.
- [ ] Ask Him to send you a Bible study partner.
- [ ] Ask God to direct you to a spiritual mentor who can disciple you in the Word.

NOTES

Lessons from the Journey

I admit it. I am hooked on texting. My cell phone and I are not easily separated. Unless I am with my friends, most all of our communication is through my phone. However, someone recently sent me an e-mail message that, while kinda lame, did make me think.

Do you ever wonder what would happen if we treated our Bibles like we treat our cell phones?

- **What IF we carried it around in our purses or pockets?**
- **What IF we flipped through it several times a day?**
- **What IF we turned back to get it if we forgot it?**
- **What IF we used it to receive messages?**
- **What IF we treated it like we couldn't live without it?**
- **What IF we gave it to kids as gifts?**
- **What IF we used it when we traveled?**
- **What IF we used it in case of an emergency?**
- **This is something to make you go, "Hmmm, where IS my Bible?"**

While I don't ever remember misplacing my cell phone for more than a few moments, there have been weeks when my Bible didn't move from the spot I put it when I came home from church until the following Sunday morning when I went looking for it.

Last year I began a regular pattern of reading the Bible and journaling. I started going to a small group where I was held accountable to read Scripture every night. I've gained a greater understanding of the importance and value of staying connected to God by reading His Word.

While I can't say I carry around my Bible like I do my phone, I can honestly say that I know where it is and it is well used.

—Anna Hastings

Junior
Franklin, Tennessee

SESSION 5

DRIVING UNDER HIS THE INFLUENCE:

Are You There Yet?

"I will indeed gather you to your fathers, and you will be gathered to your grave in peace. Your eyes will not see all the disaster that I am bringing on this place and on its inhabitants." Then they reported to the king. So the king sent [messengers] and gathered all the elders of Judah and Jerusalem. Then the king went up to the LORD's temple with all the men of Judah and the inhabitants of Jerusalem, as well as the priests and the Levites — all the people from great to small. He read in their hearing all the words of the book of the covenant that had been found in the LORD's temple. Next the king stood at his post and made a covenant in the LORD's presence to follow the LORD and to keep His commandments, His decrees, and His statutes with all his heart and with all his soul in order to carry out the words of the covenant written in this book. Then he had all those present in Jerusalem and Benjamin enter [the covenant]. So all the inhabitants of Jerusalem carried out the covenant of God, the God of their ancestors. So Josiah removed everything that was detestable from all the lands belonging to the Israelites, and he required all who were present in Israel to serve the LORD their God. Throughout his reign they did not turn aside from following the LORD God of their ancestors.

2 CHRONICLES 34:28-33

Memory Verse:

Here is your last verse. Be sure to commit it to memory.

"Do not say: I am [only] a youth, for you will go to everyone I send you to and speak whatever I tell you."—Jeremiah 1:7

Road Warrior:
Conner Cress, Changing the World

It's not often that you hear of young people changing the world for the better. To be truthful, there are not many adults changing the world for the better either.

Yet when a young man named Conner Cress, a high school student in Georgia, saw an image in a magazine of a "skeletal-looking baby, with toothpick-thin arms and legs and wide hopeless eyes," accompanied by an equally sad story about the horrific conditions in third-world countries due to poverty, starvation, and dehydration, he felt he needed to do something.

Conner recounted later that he felt the tension between his relatively carefree life as an American teenager and the survivalist life of others who lacked clean water and food.

So he brought the issue to four of his buddies — Logan, Dan, Kyle, and Jared — and together they decided to act.

Dry Tears, an organization to help provide clean drinking water to people in Africa, was formed. They chose the name to represent the lack of tears produced when someone is suffering from dehydration.

The group's website says, "Around the world, 1.1 billion people do not have access to clean water. Each day, about 6,000 people, mostly children, die from diseases related to bad or no water; that's nearly 2.2 million deaths a year."

Today, these young men have created a movement of change. They speak to schools and youth groups in their community, and they continue to raise money by selling bracelets and T-shirts to support their campaign.

Making an Impact for God

Cars don't move by themselves. Someone has to drive them. You are like a car. Every day someone or something is controlling you. You are driving through life under the influence. The question is: Which influence are you choosing?

If you have accepted Jesus as Savior, the Holy Spirit lives in you. Each morning when you wake up, someone will take control of your life. It will be either you or the Holy Spirit.

> **travel tip**
> God is far more interested in a love relationship with you than He is in what you do for Him.
> — Henry Blackaby[1]

The default setting of our lives is on self, so unless you make a conscious choice to give control over to God, you will be the driving influence. But God loves you so much that He will direct you in the ways that are best for you.

Studying the life of Josiah is challenging but also encouraging. He was a young person like you; he made some good decisions early on; he lived a life that glorified God; he changed his entire community; and he remains an example to this day.

In order to live your life and direct your destiny, it helps to start with the end in mind.

☑ Read 2 Kings 23:25. What does this verse say about Josiah's life?

Josiah was known for his stand for God! Scripture says that there was no king like him who turned to God with all of his heart. Wow! That is a pretty strong statement about someone — to be known as a man who turned to God with all his heart. All through Scripture we are introduced to people who are known for their relationship with God.

- Moses was known as the prophet "whom the L ORD knew face to face" (Deuteronomy 34:10).
- Noah was known as a man who "walked with God" (Genesis 6:9).
- Abraham was known as "God's friend" (James 2:23).
- Samuel was known as a "man of God" (1 Samuel 9:6).
- Mary was known as a "favored woman" (Luke 1:28).
- David was known as a "man after [God's] own heart" (1 Samuel 13:14, NIV).
- John was known as "the disciple whom Jesus loved" (John 21:7, NIV).

Lives that have that kind of impact are no accident. These people lived intentionally! Each of these individuals made choices that defined their destiny. Josiah made some good choices. Josiah chose to stand strong, stand up, stand on, and stand out. Let's recap the major points.

suggested tunes for the journey

Listen to "Legacy" from the *We Need Each Other* album by Sanctus Real.

Josiah Chose to STAND STRONG

[Josiah] did what was right in the L ORD's sight and walked in the ways of his ancestor David; he did not turn aside to the right or the left . . . while he was still a youth, Josiah began to seek the God of his ancestor David. (2 Chronicles 34:2-3)

From an early age, Josiah made the choice to seek God. He was determined to stand strong for what was right. He was not distracted by the "noise" around him. He was locked in on the target God set before him. He rose above circumstances—negative influences, obstacles, culture, and the crowd.

What are some things for which you have determined to take a stand? How will you be known? Use the appropriate sentence starters to consider how you would like people to remember you and your influence.

☆ I want my high school years to be represented by . . .

☆ After my college years, I want people to say . . .

☆ When my life is over, I want to be described as . . .

☆ I want to be known as a . . .

Josiah Chose to STAND UP

Josiah was passionate about his relationship with the Lord. His life was yielded to God, and that led to some big changes. It's not that he changed his behavior to fit a certain mold, but he yielded and surrendered his life to God and was changed from the inside out.

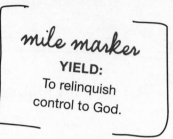

mile marker
YIELD:
To relinquish control to God.

Josiah walked away from family traditions and a heritage that denied God in order to do what was right in the eyes of the Lord. He stood up for God's holiness and launched a lifelong quest to turn his people back to God.

☑ Reread 2 Chronicles 34:4-9. These verses review what Josiah did to clean up his community.

- **He cleaned out the neighborhood.**
- **He got rid of all the religious shrines.**
- **He wrecked the altars of Baal.**
- **He tore down the altars to the pagan gods.**
- **He scattered the debris.**
- **He burned the bones of the pagan priests.**
- **He scrubbed the place clean.**
- **He cleaned up the surrounding land.**
- **He renovated the temple of God.**

What are some things you have determined to do differently as a result of studying the life of Josiah?

Josiah Chose to STAND ON

In session 4 we learned that the people had lost the Scriptures. The Word of God was not only not being used, but it was so lost that it had actually been covered with debris.

travel tip
Leaders are willing to face embarrassment or misunderstanding by others to accomplish God's purpose.
— Richard Land[2]

For years the Scriptures were ignored, and as a result of that, the people lost their way. They didn't have a reference point for what was right or wrong. They had lost hope for any righteous standard of living. Everyone did what was right in his or her own eyes.

When Josiah heard the Scriptures, he knew right away it was the Word of God. He realized that he and his people had sinned greatly against the Lord. He immediately responded and adjusted his life to God's standard.

What are some things God's Spirit has revealed to you about His Word as a result of studying the life of Josiah?

Off-Road Challenge

Many Christians base their standards for living on the world's standards. They think that if they can look and act better than most people in the world, that's good enough. The problem is that the world is always lowering its standards. If you as a believer are trying to stay just above the world, then your standards are dropping fast.

☑ Read 2 Timothy 3:1-5.

These verses describe people who are following after the world instead of God. List what they are known for:

Do the descriptions in these verses describe you?

If you say that you know God and then act this way, you are being a person who acts religious but rejects the power that makes you godly.

Take time to pray and refocus your heart on your relationship with God. Ask God to reveal anything in your life that is hindering your relationship with Him.

Josiah Chose to STAND OUT

☑ Read 2 Chronicles 34:28-33. After Josiah found the Word, he did something about it. He called all the leaders together. Check the people that he gathered:

- ☐ **Leaders**
- ☐ **Elders**
- ☐ **Citizens**
- ☐ **Families**
- ☐ **Priests**

Josiah brought a huge number of people together at the temple. What does it mean that the people were "from great to small"?

Notice what happened after the people were gathered at the temple.

☑ Read 2 Chronicles 34:31-32. What did Josiah personally do? What did he ask the people to do? Check all that apply:

- ☐ **He made a speech.**
- ☐ **He stood and publicly committed himself to God.**
- ☐ **He announced his candidacy for reelection.**
- ☐ **He renewed the covenant in the Lord's presence.**
- ☐ **He introduced his plan to start a recycling program.**
- ☐ **He pledged to obey the Lord.**
- ☐ **He introduced a new healthcare plan.**
- ☐ **He led the people to renew their covenant with God.**
- ☐ **He removed all the detestable idols from the entire land.**
- ☐ **He lowered taxes.**
- ☐ **He led everyone in worship.**

People were present from all walks of life. They had all kinds of needs, hurts, and issues. Josiah gave them exactly what they needed: the Word of God. The people hadn't heard the Word in decades. Can you imagine what that must have been like?

Josiah demonstrated good leadership principles. As soon as he received the Word, it impacted his life — and he was quick to share with others what God said.

When was the last time you received a word from God and shared it with someone else?

List three things God has recently taught or showed you.

1.

2.

3.

Scripture says that for the rest of Josiah's life, the people did not turn away from the Lord. When God saw Josiah's heart, He had compassion on him and his people.

Josiah could have found the Word, applied it to his life, and then relaxed. But he took the opportunity as a leader to share what he had learned with the rest of the people in his circle of influence. He spoke out and invited the people in his community to take a stand for God.

How are you going to use your influence for God?

Josiah made a commitment to God. Then he made it public. Josiah wasn't planning to change his mind and wimp out on his commitment. By making it public and inviting others to join him, he acquired accountability. What types of accountability do you have to help you stand strong?

travel tip
God used men and women who were dedicated to the practice of prayer to change the course of history.
— Tom Elliff[3]

Straight Ahead

Be aware that when you choose to stand strong, stand up, and stand on the Word of God, you will definitely STAND OUT. Josiah didn't have just one or two good days for God; he lived for God throughout his life.

Life is a highway that keeps on going. If you are going to live like Josiah, you need to be committed and ready.

Second Chronicles 34:33 says that Josiah didn't depart from following the Lord God for all his days. The reason you can hold up Josiah as an example to follow is because he was under the influence of the Holy Spirit.

People have others who follow them. Who follows you?

If you follow Josiah's model, you follow God. If people follow you, who else are they following?

Remember that Josiah was a young person like you. And he wasn't the only young person who made a difference by being under the influence of

God. Throughout Scripture we see God at work early in people's lives. God has accomplished His plan through the lives of many young people who stood strong.

☑ Look at what God accomplished through the life of **David**:

> *He had plans to use a young shepherd boy named David to become a great king — a man who went down in the history books as a man after God's own heart. (See 1 Samuel 16–2 Samuel 23.)*

☑ Look at what God accomplished through the life of **Joseph**:

> *He had plans to use a seventeen-year-old boy named Joseph to eventually become second in command of Egypt. (See Genesis 37–41.)*

☑ Look at what God accomplished through the life of **Daniel**:

> *He had plans to raise up a young man named Daniel, who stood strong with a commitment like none other recorded in Scripture. He was a young man of integrity who later became a statesman, a government official, and a prophet. (See Daniel 1–12.)*

☑ Look at what God accomplished through the life of **Samuel**:

> *He had plans to call Samuel as a boy to be His prophet during perhaps the most tragic time of Israel's history. (See 1 Samuel 2–25.)*

All through Scripture we see how God worked in the lives of young people like Josiah.

Scripture affirms there was no king either before or after Josiah who was more obedient to God's Law. Throughout his entire life, Josiah was committed to the work of the Lord.

Josiah left a legacy of godliness. His life impacted many. The entire culture was reformed, and people turned back to God. His destiny was defined; he invested in others; he impacted his culture; and he used his influence to bring glory to God.

☑ Review the Road Warriors who are mentioned at the beginning of each session.

Which do you like best?

Which one do you relate to most?

Do you want to see Christ make a difference in your life, the lives of your friends and family, at your school and church, and through your community and country?

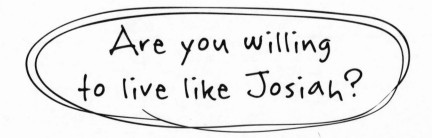

"Do not say: I am [only] a youth, for you will go to everyone I send you to and speak whatever I tell you" (Jeremiah 1:7).

Your destiny is calling. How will you answer? Prayerfully consider what commitment God is calling you to make as a result of studying Josiah's life, and write it in the space below.

Speed Bump

The road to destiny begins with a commitment. Josiah made a decision and responded quickly.

- ☐ Thank God for giving you a biblical example to follow.
- ☐ Thank God for showing you the sins that you need to avoid.
- ☐ Thank God for showing you the promises in His Word.
- ☐ Thank God for showing you what prayers to pray.
- ☐ Thank God for showing you some verses that you need to memorize.

What was the most significant statement or Scripture you read from this session?

Lessons from the Journey

During my freshman year, my walk with the Lord really hit a rough patch. I found myself choosing to study an extra half hour longer instead of having my quiet time. I couldn't find a Bible study group I was comfortable with, and I struggled to find fellow believers with whom to fellowship and be held accountable. It was one of the most spiritually dry times I had ever experienced.

As the weeks turned into months, I found myself void of all spiritual fruit. I was not loving, joyful, peaceful, or patient. Instead in my life I saw stress, anxiety, a short temper, selfishness, and an enormous lack of joy.

In the times when I did talk to God, I was selfishly asking Him to help me get an A on this test or to do really well on that paper. I didn't give even a thought to what He wanted me to do. I would get angry with God for not being close to me.

But God was faithful to me. He did not allow me to be snatched from His hand. I remember sitting in my room one night crying, asking God why He refused to be near to me. That's when it hit me — He hadn't gone anywhere. I had drifted.

"Draw near to God, and He will draw near to you," James 4:8 says. I realized that I needed to redirect my focus to God, starting with immersing myself in His Word every day. I made Him and His Word central once again. And because of that, I have joy again.

—Leah Massengill

Junior
Brentwood, Tennessee

Acknowledgments

Anyone who knows us well knows that when it comes to writing projects, we both need a lot of assistance. The fact is the Josiah Road initiative is the result of a collaborative effort that began years ago. This workbook is just one piece of the investment of many individuals. So to all those who have helped and encouraged us as this project took shape — thank you!

First of all, we'd like to thank Dr. Richard Land and Dr. Jay Strack for their support and encouragement on this project.

Thanks to Bobby Reed and the entire ERLC administrative team of Noah Braymen, Doug Carlson, Amber Chesser, Pat Clark, Marie Delph, Lucretia Goddard, Matt Hawkins, Barbara Jester, Tom Strode, Teena Thompson, Joan Stewart, and Sulyn Wilkins for their encouragement, prayers, and assistance along the way.

We would also like to express our gratitude to Karen Cole, Dwayne Hastings, Andrew Hebert, and the entire creative/editorial J-Road team of Tim Cuffman, Barrett Duke, Anna Hastings, Niles Hastings, Maston Jackson, Jody Johnston, Leah Massengill, Brian Mills, Jill Waggoner, and Rachel Wiles who played a part in the development of this project.

Claude King has been our chief encourager, prayer partner, and spiritual investor for this initiative. His valuable insight and coaching have been a gift from God!

Judy Lawson and Josh Ulmer understand our hearts and have believed in this project from the first moment we discussed it. They have played a huge part in its development. Their suggestions, insight, prayers, advice, editorial and administrative support, and assistance have been incredible. We could not have done this without their passionate work ethic!

At the heart of this initiative is our longtime friend Kerry Bural. We have been blessed by the creativity that flows from his life. We have said many times, "He is the most creative person we have ever met!" Kerry first saw the vision for Josiah Road when he heard us talking about all that God was showing us from our time of study in the Word. Thank you, Kerry, for sharing your talents with us and for bringing a creative team to the table to make it visible! We especially thank Rachel Lovingood and Michael Kelley for their assistance with the writing, and the production team of Sarah Hellems, Dustin Secrest, Jack Brannen, and Chris Boyd for their graphic and Web support.

We are especially thankful to our family: Donna (mother and wife) and Hannah (sister and daughter). They both have been incredible cheerleaders! Without their prayers, encouragement, and faithful support, this project would not have seen the light of day.

Finally, we want to thank our Lord and Savior Jesus Christ for calling us to this project. This study is His; we were just privileged to play a small part. It is our prayer that we have been the pen in His hand and that all that has been written will bring honor and glory to Him.

—Luke and Harold Harper

Scripture Memory Cards

Cut out these Scripture memory cards and carry one with you every day. Read the verse aloud several times during the day. If the verse is long, divide it into short phrases and learn to quote one phrase at a time. When you can quote one phrase word for word, add another phrase. Continue adding phrases until you can quote the entire verse or passage. When you are ready, find a friend and recite each verse. When you have a verse committed to memory, make a point to review the verse once a week for the next twelve weeks.

SESSION 1

Proverbs 3:5-6 — "Trust in the LORD with all your heart, and do not rely on your own understanding; think about Him in all your ways, and He will guide you on the right paths."

SESSION 2

John 14:26 — "But the Counselor, the Holy Spirit — the Father will send Him in My name — will teach you all things and remind you of everything I have told you."

SESSION 3

Psalm 139:23-24 — "Search me, God, and know my heart; test me and know my concerns. See if there is any offensive way in me; lead me in the everlasting way."

SESSION 4

Hebrews 4:12 — "For the word of God is living and effective and sharper than any two-edged sword, penetrating as far as to divide soul, spirit, joints, and marrow; it is a judge of the ideas and thoughts of the heart."

SESSION 5

Jeremiah 1:7 — "Do not say: I am [only] a youth, for you will go to everyone I send you to and speak whatever I tell you."

The Bridge

I. God's Love

God created us in His own image to be His friends and to experience a full life assured of His love. But He didn't make us robots. He gave us the freedom of choice.

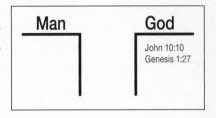

- **Q1: What do you think it means to really live life to the fullest?**
- **Q2: How are God and mankind different?**

II. Man's Problem

Mankind has chosen to disobey God and thus become separated from Him. The penalty of this separation is eternal spiritual death.

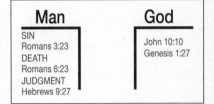

- **Q3: Have you ever wanted to talk to God but He seemed far away?**
- **Q4: When you think of death, what do you think of?**

III. God's Remedy

On our own, we cannot attain the perfection needed to bridge the gap between mankind and God. Christ's death alone is adequate for our sin and bridges the gulf between God and man.

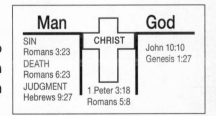

- **Q5: If death can be defined as separation from God, what is life?**
- **Q6: Why did Christ die?**

IV. Man's Response

Believing means trust and commitment — acknowledging our sinfulness, trusting Christ's forgiveness, and letting Him control our life. Eternal life is a gift for us to receive.

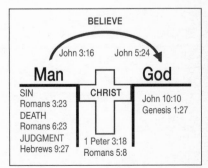

- **Q7: Where would you place yourself in this illustration?**
- **Q8: Is there any reason you shouldn't cross over to God's side and be certain of eternal life?**

Group Contact Information

Name _____ Number _____

E-mail _____

Name _____ Number _____

E-mail _____

Name _____ Number _____

E-mail _____

Name _____ Number _____

E-mail _____

Name _____ Number _____

E-mail _____

Name _____ Number _____

E-mail _____

Name _____ Number _____

E-mail _____

Name _____ Number _____

E-mail _____

Name _____ Number _____

E-mail _____

Name _____ Number _____

E-mail _____

Name _____ Number _____

E-mail _____

Name _____ Number _____

E-mail _____

Name _____ Number _____

E-mail _____

Notes

Session 1

1. Adapted from *Baptist Press* (March 2, 2007) and the *Florida Baptist Witness* (February 15, 2007).
2. Andy Stanley and Stuart Hall, *Max Q: Developing Students of Influence* (West Monroe, LA: Howard Publishing, 2004), 19.
3. John C. Maxwell, *Developing the Leader Within You* (Nashville: Thomas Nelson, 1993), 2.
4. Pat Williams and Jay Strack, *The Three Success Secrets of Shamgar* (Deerfield Beach, FL: Faith Communications, 2004), 190–193.
5. Williams and Strack, 190–193.
6. Williams and Strack, 190–193.
7. Williams and Strack, 190–193.
8. Adapted from Richard and Henry Blackaby and Claude King, *Experiencing God: Knowing and Doing the Will of God* (Nashville: LifeWay, rev. 2007), 11–15.

Session 2

1. Adapted from *Baptist Press* (May 11, 2009).
2. Adapted from Claude King, *The Call to Follow Christ* (Nashville: LifeWay, 2006), 26–27.
3. King, 26–27.
4. King, 26–27.
5. Adapted from *KNOWN* 02, Student Curriculum, vol. 1, no. 5 (Nashville: LifeWay, January 2009), 20.

Session 3

1. Richard Land, *Imagine! A God Blessed America: What It Would Look Like and How It Could Happen* (Nashville: Broadman & Holman, 2005), 110.
2. Henry Blackaby and Claude King, *Fresh Encounter: Experiencing God Through Prayer, Humility, and a Heartfelt Desire to Know Him* (Nashville: Broadman & Holman, 1996), 81.
3. Adapted from Claude King, *The Call to Follow Christ* (Nashville: LifeWay, 2006), 14.
4. John MacArthur, *Christ Displays His Glory* (Chicago: Moody, 1987).
5. King, 14.

Session 4

1. To find out more about The Rebelution, visit www.therebelution.com.
2. Adapted from Henry and Richard Blackaby and Claude King, *Experiencing God: Knowing and Doing the Will of God* (Nashville: LifeWay, rev. 2007), 126.
3. Adapted from a sermon delivered by Andy Stanley: Breaking with Tradition: Part Three, "One Man's Journey," available online from North Point resources.
4. Howard Hendricks, *Living by the Book* (Chicago: Moody, 1991), 18.
5. Inspired by *KNOWN* 02, Student Curriculum, vol. 1, no. 5, "Meditate on God's Word" (Nashville: LifeWay, January 2009), 21.

Session 5

1. Adapted from Henry and Richard Blackaby and Claude King, *Experiencing God: Knowing and Doing the Will of God* (Nashville: LifeWay, rev. 2007), 52.
2. Richard Land, *Imagine! A God Blessed America: What It Would Look Like and How It Could Happen* (Nashville: Broadman & Holman, 2005), 111.
3. Tom Elliff, *A Passion for Prayer* (Wheaton, IL: Crossway, 1998), 17.

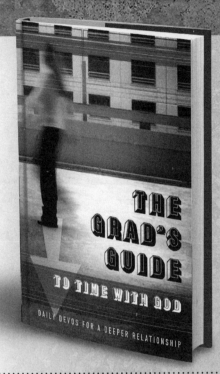
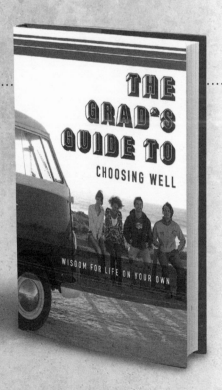

MY LIFE IS **TOUGHER** THAN MOST **PEOPLE REALIZE.**

I TRY TO KEEP EVERYTHING **IN BALANCE:** FRIENDS, FAMILY, WORK, SCHOOL, AND GOD.

IT'S NOT EASY.

I KNOW WHAT MY PARENTS BELIEVE AND WHAT MY PASTOR SAYS.

BUT IT'S NOT ABOUT THEM. IT'S ABOUT ME...

ISN'T IT TIME I OWN MY FAITH?

THROUGH THICK AND THIN, KEEP YOUR HEARTS AT ATTENTION, IN ADORATION BEFORE CHRIST, YOUR MASTER. BE READY TO SPEAK UP AND TELL ANYONE WHO ASKS WHY YOU'RE LIVING THE WAY YOU ARE, AND ALWAYS WITH THE UTMOST COURTESY. 1 PETER 3:15 (MSG)

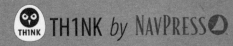

www.navpress.com | 1-800-366-7788

TH1NK by NAVPRESS

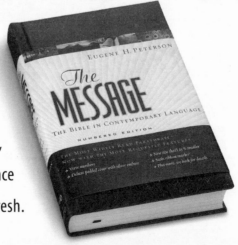

NavPress - A Ministry of The Navigators

*Wherever you are in your spiritual journey,
NavPress will help you grow.*

The NavPress mission is to advance the calling of The Navigators by publishing life-transforming products that are biblically rooted, culturally relevant, and highly practical.